Rosemary's Ramblings

– WRITTEN BY ROSEMARY SOLOMON –
– COVER ILLUSTRATION BY HARRIET RUSSELL –

An environmentally friendly book printed and bound in England by
www.printondemand-worldwide.com

Mixed Sources
Product group from well-managed
forests, and other controlled sources
www.fsc.org Cert no. TT-COC-002641
© 1996 Forest Stewardship Council

FSC

PEFC Certified
This product is
from sustainably
managed forests
and controlled
sources
www.pefc.org

PEFC
PEFC/16-33-415

This book is made entirely of chain-of-custody materials

www.fast-print.net/store.php

ROSEMARY'S RAMBLINGS
Copyright © Rosemary Solomon 2013

A catalogue record for this book is available from the British Library

ISBN 978-178035-732-4

First published 2013 by
FASTPRINT PUBLISHING
Peterborough, England.

Dedication

This book is dedicated to my two amazing daughters, Ruth and Anne, who have encouraged me throughout and allowed me to write about them. To my dog, Blackie, who has not given me permission to write about his antics, but I did anyway, and to God for inspiring me with ideas.

To Betty.

Every blessing

Rosemary

Rosemary Solomon

Introduction

The concept of writing *Rosemary's Ramblings* was officially born when I came into ministry in 1999. They came out of an expectation that I would write something for the Church magazine and they have developed from life's experience.

The gift of life is a very special gift, but just like any present sometimes it is wrapped in pretty paper and sometimes it turns up in a shabby box. I believe that God is there with us, whatever life presents us with and however it does so.

I've been a Christian all my life, but there have been plenty of ups and downs and times when I've walked away from God. Yet somehow God always manages to call me back.

Training for ministry was not ever part of my plan. In fact I questioned my calling for many years, convinced that God had made a mistake. But I have come to realise that God doesn't get it wrong. Rather He has given me a gift – the gift of writing; the gift of seeing God in the everyday.

I have had so much fun writing these Ramblings. I hope I will continue to ramble for many years to come. More importantly I hope you will enjoy reading them.

Some members of my congregations might recognise themselves in the stories, although they are deliberately kept anonymous.

Whether you recognise yourselves or not, I hope you will see parallels with your life in these stories, that they will make you smile, and I pray they will bring you closer to God.

Contents

1	How big are your feet?	11
2	Getting old	13
3	Looking after hamsters	15
4	The joy of knitting	17
5	Sand between your toes	19
6	The Wasjig	21
7	Recording for local radio	23
8	Carrying too much weight	25
9	Needing an eye test	27
10	When were you born?	29
11	Getting out of your depth	31
12	Keeping in touch with God	33
13	Special celebrations	35
14	Stereotypes	37
15	Keeping active	39
16	God's time versus our time	41
17	Wearing glasses	43
18	The colour of underwear	45
19	The story of the disappearing piece of cheese	47
20	Problem phones	49
21	Understanding time	51
22	Joining the gym	53
23	The jigsaw puzzle	55
24	A muddy walk	57
25	Making noises	59
26	Sharpened pencils	61
27	Using all our senses	63

28	A birthday cake	65
29	Putting others first	67
30	Coming up slowly	69
31	Remembering names	71
32	Walking the dog	73
33	What's in your bag?	75
34	Changing fashions	77
35	Recycling our "rubbish"?	79
36	Keeping your options open	81
37	Jagged edges	83
38	Losing sight of God	85
39	The Christmas amaryllis	87
40	The innocence of a child	89
41	Being in control	91
42	Black teeth	93
43	Honeymoon gifts	95
44	The dog and the cushion	97
45	Teaching Murphy recall	99

How big are your feet?

I was coming towards the end of my first pregnancy when, having waddled along for my regular check-up at the antenatal clinic, I was surprised when the doctor asked me to take off my shoes so he could look at my feet. Now, as every mum or mum-to-be will tell you, feet disappear around the sixth month, along with anything resembling a lap, and the dressing and undressing of feet, plus the cutting of toenails, is usually done by guesswork or with the help of a sympathetic partner.

The clinic's staff were normally far more concerned with blood pressure and whether you had remembered to bring your sample. Still, who was I to question? So I obligingly struggled to remove my shoes, exposing my tiny size fours.

"Hmm," he said in that clinical voice, which seems to come as standard equipment to all in the medical profession. "I think this baby will have to be born by Caesarean section."

Funny things, feet. Whilst we long to be taller or shorter, change the colour of our hair and struggle with diets and exercise to reduce the size of our thighs, flatten our stomachs or increase our biceps, we pay little attention to our feet, hiding them away and only remembering them when they hurt.

Of course, in Jesus' time it was very different. When a friend calls to see me now I offer a cup of coffee or tea, but then the number one priority would be to attend to the needs of their feet. A host would be considered most rude if a bowl of water and a towel were not provided.

Such a practice may seem very strange to us today. But perhaps we should take better care of our feet; we can't go anywhere without them. I can't change the size of my feet but what I can do is make sure that I walk firmly and confidently in the footsteps that Jesus has left for me to follow. Like the servant in the carol *Good King Wenceslas*, our journey will be easier if we tread in our Master's steps.

Oh, by the way, the doctor was right: I did need a Caesarean. I wonder how he could tell that just by looking at my feet!

Getting old

One of the problems with the ageing process, as I am beginning to discover, is bits start to wear out. Hearing decreases, eyesight isn't as sharp as it was, and knees and hips twinge on a regular basis.

Of course, medical science has moved on substantially and many of our bits and pieces, such as knees and hips, can be replaced while glasses and hearing aids can help other problems. Unfortunately, as far as I am aware, science hasn't yet developed the capacity to improve my diminishing muscle tone and suppleness.

You know it's happening when getting up from a chair takes more effort than it used to and, when you bend down to retrieve something from the floor, you have to enlist the help of someone else to bend down and retrieve you!

But I refuse to give in, well not yet anyway, so I am working with a combination of swimming and some general stretching exercises. And I'm pleased to say it's making a difference. My back and shoulders are much more supple and just a few gentle exercises a day mean I can stretch further than I used to.

Rosemary Solomon

Every little helps. Even just a little exercise every now and then makes a difference to your overall health and feeling of wellbeing.

And so it is with God. Just a little bit of God every day will make a positive difference to your life and your general wellbeing.

Of course, I don't always feel like swimming, and sometimes I'm really too busy to be bothered with my exercises, but I always feel better for them and I do miss them when they don't happen. In the same way, it can be hard to find time for God, but having God in your life does make a difference and skipping God will leave an emptiness that is impossible to fill with anything else.

Looking after hamsters

There was an occasion, when my daughter was younger, when I was required to temporarily look after her two hamsters.

I have to be honest and say I am not really a small furry pet person but, to be fair, these two rodents were good entertainment value, in a nocturnal sort of way.

They, Ginger and Twiglet, generally appeared during the late evening and their main activity involved climbing up the side of the cage and hanging from the roof upside down – a tricky manoeuvre which inevitably resulted in them falling off.

When they were not hanging from the roof, they liked to use their wheel, which is when I would feel sorry for them, because they would spend hours and hours running their little legs off and getting absolutely nowhere.

Do you ever feel like that? Do you have days when it feels like you have been on the go all day, but when you stop and reflect you feel you have achieved nothing?

I guess the hamster doesn't have much of a choice. For him (or her) it's the wheel or nothing. But we are different. We do have choices and we can broaden our horizons if we wish. We can commit our lives to God, rising to the challenges that such a commitment requires, or we can remain contained in the narrowness of our lives, going nowhere and achieving nothing.

The joy of knitting

I like knitting!

Many years ago, when we lived in Southampton, there was a very good wool shop just at the edge of the shopping precinct. As well as selling balls of wool in every shape, size and colour you could possibly imagine, the shop also had some large bins full of skeins of wool. They were always cheaper than the regular balls of wool and if you had the time and the patience to wind the skeins into balls, you could pick up a real bargain.

It so happened that whilst I was pregnant with our first baby, the shop suddenly produced a whole bin full of baby wool – skeins and skeins of pinks, lemons and blues but, somewhat predictably, very little white. Well, always one for a bargain I rummaged my way down to the very bottom of the bin and found a large skein of white baby wool. The only problem was whereas all the other skeins just needed to be wound into balls, this skein of white wool was tangled beyond belief.

I was about to put it back when the assistant offered, "You can have that for nothing, it's so badly tangled, I can't sell that."

You know how it is, you always intend to do something, but somehow events overtake you, and although I found time to wind and knit the other colours into baby clothes, I couldn't face tackling the tangled mess of white wool.

Then an elderly friend, also an accomplished knitter, came to visit. Her eyes fell on the tangled heap of white wool.

"Give me that," she said. "I will knit it into a shawl."

To be honest, I thought she was joking but, sure enough, when Ruth was born, my friend presented us with the most beautiful, delicate, knitted shawl. I was amazed.

"It must have taken you hours to untangle the wool, never mind knit the shawl."

"Well my dear," she replied. "It did take a long time to unravel the mess. I could only manage a little every day but, bit by bit, the pile of chaos grew less and eventually I was able to create something very special out of it."

Sometimes I think God must look at our tangled lives and sigh a big sigh. How did we get in such a mess? But if we allow Him to, God will untangle the mess we have made of our lives, little by little, a bit every day and create something very special.

Sand between your toes

With the lighter evenings and the odd hint of warm spring sunshine, our thoughts inevitably start to turn towards the promise of summer, and in particular summer holidays.

Warm, sunny days and sandy beaches spring to mind as we look forward to a time of relaxation and an opportunity to recharge flagging batteries. And whether we regard a holiday as a time to be particularly active and enjoy more energetic pastimes, such as rock climbing or white-water rafting, or whether we would rather relax in a chair in the sun with a cool drink, there is always the opportunity to marvel at nature and God's creation.

Nature is stunning and amazing all in one go. It's not just nature's beauty that touches me, it is also the way nature lives in harmony and the way nature uses itself to good advantage.

In the Bible Jesus likens the Kingdom of Heaven to, amongst other things, a precious pearl. A pearl is without doubt a thing of great beauty but we need to learn from nature just how pearls form. They start with a tiny speck of grit that finds its way inside oysters. Basically, that speck of grit is a nuisance, an irritant – think how you feel when you get a piece of dirt or grit in your eye, or between your toes. Yet the oyster takes that which is troublesome and turns it into something that is special beyond price.

Likewise, God will take that which is troublesome about us and work with us to turn that nuisance, that irritant, into something good. But only if we let him.

The Wasgij

In amongst other things, I bought my daughter's boyfriend a jigsaw puzzle for Christmas. Nothing particularly amazing about that, you may think, but this was a jigsaw puzzle with a difference. It's called a Wasgij and the difference is that the picture of the puzzle on the box is not the picture of the puzzle in the box. The picture on the box merely gives clues as to what is contained within. The person attempting to complete the puzzle needs, first of all, to try to answer the clues to get some idea of what they are aiming for.

Life, it seems to me, resembles a jigsaw puzzle. The four corners, which are the pieces you normally locate first when attempting to build a puzzle, represent the foundations of our lives. These are our building blocks, the criteria from which we build our personal framework. Just as we move on from the four corners of the puzzle to find all the straight-edged pieces, so in life we grow out from our foundations. Having created the framework, we are then faced with the joy or challenge of fitting all the pieces into the picture.

The placing of some pieces is obvious – some pieces go together to make a small picture or shape, and we often find ourselves with several disjointed groups of pieces: each a whole in its own right, but dependent on being connected with all the other pieces in order to make sense and be complete.

Sometimes, or rather often, there are pieces that look identical, a blue sky, or a swathe of green grass. It is hard to know exactly where they fit. We can only establish the correct place by trial and error and making many mistakes as we test out where a particular piece goes. In our lives too, we often have to make mistakes in order to establish a way forward as we struggle to make sense of what is going on.

And, like the person completing a Wasgij, we are attempting to build the picture, which is our lives, without any prior knowledge of what that picture actually looks like. The best we can hope for are clues to help us along the way.

Our clues come from God. For God is the only one who knows what the completed picture should look like and God is the only one who can help us.

Recording for local radio

Recording for radio programmes is a strange experience. As part of one of my ministries, I was invited by the local radio station to record seven two-minute *Thought For The Day* type talks.

My first experience in a recording studio was scary. Having been ushered into a tiny room, huge headphones were placed over my ears and a large microphone was gently pushed to be almost touching my nose. For a few seconds all was quiet then the voice of the person in charge jumped out at me through my headphones. Having tested the sound levels he gave the instruction to speak into the microphone when I was ready and then left me to get on with it.

It felt mildly uncomfortable, holding a conversation with myself, taking into nothingness, completely shut off from the outside world, with the sensitivity of the microphone echoing my voice back to me. I completed all of my seven pieces and waited. Nothing happened.

"Erm, that's it," I mumbled somewhat stupidly into the mic.

There were a few more seconds of silence then, just as I was wondering if anyone was actually there, the voice of the person in charge boomed out at me, still through my headphones, "Thank you, Rosemary, that's fine."

As someone used to talking face-to-face to a person or, if nothing else, a voice at the end of the phone, it felt odd just to chatter away without response. But then praying can often feel like that. Shut away somewhere quiet, as we try to distance ourselves from the busyness of reality, it can seem as though we are talking to thin air, and we can be forgiven for wondering if anyone is really listening.

I say what I want to say – and there is silence – and I return to the daily routine. Yet God, the person in charge, is listening. We may not always be aware and it may sometimes take a little while before we hear His voice, but be assured, God does respond in the way that He knows is right for us.

Carrying too much weight

Confession time. Did you put on weight over Christmas? Did you promise yourself you would lose it early in the New Year? Do you still need to lose that weight?

It would, of course, be foolish to ask why we put on weight. In the main it's because we have eaten too much. We have simply been unable to resist the temptation of saying yes to an extra piece of cake or a large slice of pie when a small slice would have been perfectly adequate, and the price we pay for our folly is an additional burden in the guise of too many pounds.

We've all done it. Eaten an overly large meal and then sat in a chair feeling uncomfortably bloated. Happily, the odd indulgence won't do us too much damage, but if we continue to eat more than we should then the scales cannot deny the horrible truth. And even if we refuse to check the scales the very fact that our clothes are becoming too tight is a good indication that we have been less than sensible.

Being overweight is not good for our health in the long term. You don't need me to remind you that carrying too much weight puts pressure on the heart, the joints, and the lungs until ultimately our health is in great danger.

"God never gives us more than we cope with."

That statement turned up recently in my book of daily devotions. It made me think of how easy it is, especially when we are struggling with something, to take the whole problem and then wonder why we feel so "weighed down". If only we could take just a slice – try to cope with a manageable portion – we might even find, when we are ready to go back for another helping, that others have taken a slice in the meantime, thus considerably reducing what we first saw as such a major issue.

Lent is traditionally the time to give something up. When we approach Lent this year let's try to give up taking too much. Let's try to keep ourselves, not just physically, but spiritually healthy for God.

Needing an eye test

I really must get my eyes tested!

Someone once told me the best way to judge a person's age is to measure how far away he or she needs to hold something before they can read it. When you get to the point that your arms just aren't long enough, old age has really set in.

But for me, it's not just about the length of my arms. I was born with an eye defect, which resulted in specs since I was just 18 months old and surgery when I was three. That, coupled with glaucoma in the close family, means I'm supposed to get my eyes tested on an annual basis.

Of course, even given the defect, my eyesight has deteriorated with age. When I was a vain teenager far more interested in my appearance and, more specifically, how I looked to boys, I would happily walk home from school without my glasses. I couldn't do that now. Well, I proved that on the day that I almost got into the local swimming pool when it still had its cover on. I did think that the water was particularly blue that morning!

Anyway, I think it could well be time for new glasses this time round. The current ones are four years old and I know there has been a slight change in the prescription, so I'm hoping that some new lenses will help the world to become a little clearer.

Having God in our lives also helps the way we see the world to become a little clearer. I doubt I will ever be able to view things through God's eyes, but at least if we try to see things as God does, it changes our perception dramatically and helps us to make sense of what we see in front of us.

When were you born?

Does it matter when you're born?

I was born at the end of August. The debate about whether August babies get a raw deal when it comes to education, since they end up in a class with children who can be almost a whole year older than they are, has gone on for years. I think it made a difference to me because I had to skip a whole year in primary school and I can remember still being 15 when I took my O-levels, whilst my friend was almost 17 when she took hers.

My dad was born on the first of January – which he hated. In his view his birthday came far too close to Christmas and he regularly suggested that he, like the Queen, should have an 'official' birthday later in the year.

Which brings me to another example of your birth date making a difference: I guess an April birthday isn't really conducive to good weather, especially when it comes to public events, so the present Queen has an official birthday in June. Mind you, the weather in June isn't always conducive to public events either.

And of course, if you read your horoscope, then the date of your birth matters, as it will determine your birth sign.

In December, we celebrate the birth of Jesus. Christmas Day, the 25th of December, is the day we set aside to remember the story of the nativity and the birth of

Christ. However, biblical scholars will tell you that it is highly unlikely that Jesus was born on the 25th of December; it is far more likely that he arrived at the end of September.

But what really matters is not when he was born, but the fact that he was born and the difference his life has made to our world.

And following that example, it matters not when we were born, rather the fact that we were born and the difference our lives can make to our world truly matters.

Getting out of your depth

A few years ago I was fortunate enough to go to South Africa for a holiday, where I had the opportunity to go snorkelling. Now, I am not a good swimmer but the guide assured me that even non-swimmers could manage and since I had a suspicion that this was a once-in-a-lifetime chance, I wasn't going to miss out.

I togged up with a mask and snorkel and walked with dignity into the crystal-clear water.

"The best place to snorkel is just over here by the rocks," called out the ever-helpful instructor. Well, whilst I remain convinced that he was right, what he neglected to point out was that the depth of water "just over here by the rocks" was somewhere around six feet. I could not swim out of my depth and I'm only five feet one!

Panic set in and in my desperation not to drown, I grabbed the nearest thing to me, which happened to be my youngest daughter, Anne. As I struggled to come up for air, I simply pushed my poor daughter further and further under the water. It was a close run thing but luckily we both survived (and laugh about it now!) but when back in England and on dry land I suggested that perhaps it was about time I learnt to swim out of my depth.

Anne, for some inexplicable reason, thought that was a very good idea. She even offered to help me – mainly by prising my white knuckles from the side of the pool whilst offering the encouraging suggestion that, "You won't drown and, even if you do, a handsome lifeguard will jump in and save you."

Her patience with me was worthwhile because I am pleased to say that whilst not a strong swimmer, I now have sufficient confidence to swim out of my depth. If I'm honest I would still much rather be able to swim in water where I know I can touch the bottom, but the sensation of being held up by the water is truly amazing.

Life can sometimes reach a point where we feel out of depth. The trick is to give it to God and in so doing to allow God to keep us afloat. Whatever happens, God won't let us drown; we just have to trust Him.

Keeping in touch with God

Modern technology is all very well so long as:

a. It's working, and
b. You know how to use it.

The sales assistant in a local department store the other day was doing just fine on the ordering and collection desk until her computer froze and she was left in a flustered heap, unable to process anyone's requests and with a queue of increasingly impatient customers growing by the minute.

When I was a kid we had a police telephone box on the corner opposite my house. For those of you too young to be familiar with such items, they resembled Doctor Who's TARDIS, except they worked – not in a time machine fashion, but to alert the local policeman to a phone call. When the phone was ringing inside the box, the blue light on the roof flashed on and off, alerting the local bobby to the fact that someone was trying to contact him.

I have to say it must have been a fairly hit-and-miss system, which relied on the policeman happening to pass by at just the right time or, I suppose, phoning in to his base every now and again to see if anyone had needed to get in touch with him.

I remember when my eldest daughter set off to Africa for her gap year, back in the late 1990s, the only way to communicate with her was by fax.

When fax machines first appeared, everyone held their breath with excitement. But now we have smartphones, internet, e-mails and a whole variety of other bits and pieces of technology, all designed to ensure that communication is not only instant, but also available to us wherever we are in the world and whoever we are trying to contact.

But there remains only one way to communicate with God and that is through prayer. And, of course, we can chose to communicate with God whenever the fancy takes us: In the middle of the night when we can't sleep, when we have an odd five minutes and we just can't think of anything else to do, or during a planned quiet time.

Communication, however, is a two-way thing. It's all very well for us to decide when and where we are going to get in touch, but what about if God wants to talk to us?

Whether a flashing blue light, the ping of a text or the ring of a phone – are you listening out for when He is trying to reach you?

Special celebrations

I celebrate my birthday at the end of August.

When I was a child I hated having a birthday in the summer holidays because I always felt I missed out. I never got the opportunity to take my cards into school and show them to my friends, and as for trying to organise a party it always seemed to coincide with everyone else being away.

But in adulthood, things have changed. I have really enjoyed celebrating my birthdays and have done all sorts of different and fun things. A few years ago, my two daughters invited me to spend a weekend with them in London.

I had a fantastic time. We went on a fast boat up the Thames from Greenwich to the centre of London. We went up the Monument. We saw *Calendar Girls* on the stage and between all that we managed to consume a small amount of coffee, food and wine! It was lovely to see them and to enjoy a rare opportunity for the three of us to get together.

And the question everyone asked me, after the event, was "Was it a special birthday?" by which I assume they meant "Did it have a nought at the end of it?". No it didn't and I think it is sad the way birthdays these days only seem to be special if they mark the start of a new decade in our lives.

The chance to spend time with my daughters was really good and the occasion of my birthday offered an excellent reason, because all birthdays are special – or they should be.

So it is with our time with God. There can be a tendency to think that Sunday is God's day. Well, yes it is, but so is every other day of the week, and we do not need to wait for that 'special' day in order to be with God. For every day is special and is an opportunity to be close to the God that loves us and created us.

Stereotypes

As part of my ministry, I have, from time to time, delved into teaching in local schools. And part of that teaching experience was leading lessons known as 'Personal and Social Health Education'. The theme for one of these lessons was stereotypes. So we started with a question and answer session.

I asked the class, "What does the word 'teenager' conjure up in your mind?"

Back came the responses: "Spotty, lazy, baggy trousers, loud-mouthed."

"How about 'the elderly'?"

"Wrinkled, weak, sleepy, smokes a pipe."

Of course, we know that sweeping generalisations are always dangerous and we also know that it is just not true that all teenagers are spotty, lazy, loud-mouthed and wear baggy trousers. Nor is it true that all people over a certain age are wrinkled, weak, sleepy and pipe smokers. But that is what society thinks. And I guess somewhere back in the dim and distant past there were sufficient teenagers (and elderly folk) who publicly fitted that description so well that it stuck. Which is a shame, because once a reputation is in place it is extraordinarily difficult to lose it.

I also tried the word 'vicar' on the boys.

"Holy, kind, well-behaved children, doesn't drink," and "Dibley" were the responses.

So what would society's response be to the word 'Christian'? Jesus sandals, flowery skirts, holier-than-thou do-gooder? If that would be society's stereotypical response – and I think it probably would – then the next question is why? Why, where and how have Christians gathered that kind of reputation?

So be brave. Ask your friends, neighbours, work colleagues – especially those who aren't Christians – what the term Christian conjures up in their minds. And then have the courage to face that stereotypical reputation and change people's minds.

Keeping active

I have given in. I finally accept the fact that I am getting old.

How do I know? Is it the grey hairs? Is it the extra wrinkles? Is it the natural force of gravity encouraging several of my bits and pieces to be closer to the ground than they were previously? No, it's none of those things.

So what has made me come to terms with the mind-blowing revelation that I am not as young as I used to be? It is my teenage daughter getting ready to go out for the evening when I am going to bed!

I mean, for goodness sake, how can anyone start to think about a social life at 10pm?

So that's it then. It's comfy slippers and a warm bedtime drink, varicose veins and a walking frame for me. I guess that's all there is left to look forward to. After all, it goes without saying that as I grow older not only will my hair lose its colour and my skin its elasticity, but my joints will seize up and I will become slower – because that's what happens as the body ages, isn't it?

So, how come every once in a while I meet a really sprightly eighty or even ninety year-old who continues to enjoy life and live life to the full, without even a hint of slowing down either physically or mentally? Well, nine times out of ten it's because that's how they have always lived their lives; they enjoyed plenty of exercise, a sensible diet and a good helping of mental stimulation to keep their brain active.

Anyone who has ever suffered the misfortune of breaking an arm or a leg will know how quickly the muscles in the limb will waste because they're not being used. Remove the plaster and the damaged arm or leg will appear only half the size of the good one, simply because it hasn't been used for a while. The same is true for all of us. The less we use our brains or our bodies, the quicker they will decline.

And the same is true of our spirituality. If we stop walking our Christian journey – if we stop exercising our faith – it too will wither and die. We all know the advantage of keeping our minds and our bodies active. Let's not forget the spiritual side of our being as well.

God's time versus our time

I wouldn't say I'm a creature of habit, but 10.30am is coffee time.

Monday is usually my day in the study for catching up on paperwork and starting to prepare the service for the following Sunday. On one particular Monday, I had gotten off to a good start and I was pleased with the progress that I had made during the early part of the morning. You know how it is, occasionally things go really well and when I noticed that the clock on the study windowsill was fast approaching 10.30, I knew I had earned my break. So, it was time to wander into the kitchen to find a cup of coffee and a biscuit.

When I opened the kitchen door, I couldn't believe my eyes. The clock on the kitchen wall said five to eleven! I went back to the study and double-checked the clock in there. No, that one definitely said half past ten. I consulted the clock on the television, the central heating boiler and the cooker; they all said five to eleven.

My elation turned to despair as the awful truth sunk in. The clock in the study was slow and I was almost half an hour late. My entire day was ruined! From that point onwards, everything went rapidly downhill. Somehow I couldn't persuade my brain that I hadn't actually done any less work – I had simply stopped for coffee slightly later than I would normally.

No. My coffee break was now too close to lunch. Lunch felt too early and then the afternoon suddenly became rushed. My mood swung around completely and by the end of the day I was just cross. And all for the sake of half an hour.

Time, our time, has a horrible habit of tying us up in so many knots from which we are unable to free ourselves. Time, our time, controls our lives.

If we must let time rule our lives, then let's at least try to make sure that it is God's time to which we work and not ours. More than that, try to make sure that you have time for God in each one of your days.

Wearing glasses

I hate wearing glasses! I suppose it's really something I should be used to by now, since I have worn them ever since I was just 18 months old. Initially to correct long sight and, from the age of three, to cope with a squint brought on by a bad attack of measles. Even surgery didn't take me to a place of 20/20 vision so it's been glasses ever since, and with the onset of deterioration by age, there is no chance that I will ever lose the specs now.

I hate them because they are really hot and uncomfortable when the weather is warm. I hate them because they steam up when I go from the cold outside into a warm room.

I hate them because they get grubby and every now and then I realise I am looking at the world through a fog, and they need cleaning.

Mind you, once clean the difference is amazing as the world and everything in it suddenly appears so much cleaner and sharper.

But that's a big advantage: having to clean them. It reminds me that sometimes our take on life can become cloudy and distorted. Sometimes the things of the world, or just life's downs rather than ups, make it difficult for us to see life as God would have us see it, through the eyes of Christ.

My vision will never be perfect but at least my glasses remind me that we all need to clean the muck and grime away every now and again. Only then can we clearly see God.

The colour of underwear

It's not often I get to talk about underwear, and even less frequent that I get to write about it. Of course, like all mums, my mum encouraged me to wear clean (and respectable) underwear just in case I got run over! But by and large underwear is something that we wear – I hope – but don't generally chat too much about.

Now, I like to look good. I like to be co-ordinated in what I wear and I spare a bit of thought when it comes to matching jewellery and accessories. But even I was surprised when someone (who will remain nameless to protect her modesty) told me that, as a younger woman, she always matched the colour of her underwear to her outfit. Purple skirt – purple knickers, I guess!

All of which made me stop and think, not so much about the colour of my underwear, but about how we present ourselves to the outside world. In many ways, it doesn't matter what is going on beneath the layers, so long as we look pretty clean and presentable on the top.

God, however, isn't bothered about the outside appearance.

The Lord does not look at the things man looks at. Man looks at the outward appearance, but the Lord looks at the heart.

1 Samuel 16:7 (New Life Version)

God really isn't fussed whether we are black or white, tall or short, young or old. What God is interested in is the person within. God is interested in the 'how'. How we feel, how we love, how we treat other people.

I particularly like the words of the Communion service that says, "God welcomes us, whoever we are and whatever we bring, and He will feed us at His table. Old or young, rich or poor, joyful or in sorrow, God invites us to eat with Him."

All God asks is that we treat other people in the same way.

The story of the disappearing piece of cheese

One of the biggest problems about living on your own is shopping – and more specifically shopping for food. What I have discovered over the last few years is that so many things come in large packs, designed for families, or 'buy one get one half price' offers.

There is just me at home now, so there are many things that I no longer buy. Eggs – I only want a couple, not half a dozen; celery – unless I'm prepared to eat a stick for breakfast, lunch and supper, five days in a row – and cheese. I don't eat much cheese, so even a small piece runs the risk of going mouldy before I finish it. But the other day, on a whim, I decided to treat myself to a nice piece of cheese - white Stilton with ginger and mango.

I swear I only left the kitchen for a minute. I think I just went to the bedroom to retrieve a tissue. But by the time I had returned, Blackie, my dog, had sniffed out the cheese from his position of laziness on his bed in the lounge, removed said cheese from kitchen and was currently slobbering over his prize on his bed.

It was no good being cross. He works on a 'see it, eat it' mentality. He likes cheese too and he didn't know that this cheese had my name on it and not his. He is a dog. He doesn't understand right from wrong as we do.

Of course, the whole debate over MPs' expenses has long since ceased to hit the news. The media has moved on now to other things. But the one thing that struck me when publicity was at its height was the number of people quoted as saying, "I haven't done anything wrong".

God gives us free will and freedom of choice and within that freedom we have the opportunity to identify what is right and what is not. Just because a system is there, whatever that system might be, it is up to us to first judge whether that system is right and then whether or not we wish to be a party to it.

The responsibility is ours. We know what is right and we know what is wrong, and the decisions we make are up to us.

Problem phones

Have you ever had a problem with your phone?

For me, it happened without warning. I went to make a phone call, dialled the number, heard the phone ringing at the other end but then, just at the point when the person I was calling lifted their receiver to answer, it all went horribly dead. Or at least, it didn't quite go completely dead, that was the funny thing. Sure, I couldn't hear anyone speaking to me yet at the same time I was aware of something which I can only describe as a sensation on the other end of the phone that assured me I could be heard, even though I couldn't hear anything at all.

It seemed rather foolish to be talking into the ether. But once I realised what was happening, I knew I could make a call, leave a message at the point when the person I was calling answered their phone, then put my phone down - as it were - and patiently wait for the person I was trying to contact to phone me back.

It worked like a charm. My phone could happily receive incoming calls, so when it rang, I was usually greeted with, "Hi, I knew it was you, I could hear you speaking – I could hear every word you said."

Sometimes, often, my prayers seem to me to be like the one-way conversations I was having on my phone. I come to God, dial his number, prepare what I want to say, but the minute He connects with me, I am unable to hear His voice. I'm sure He is there because the line isn't dead – there is that same sensation on the other end. But all I can do is leave a brief message for God and wait patiently for Him to come back to me.

It worked every time with my phone. If we learn to be patient, it will work every time with God.

Understanding time

When I was a child, I found it hard to understand how my grandparents could hold in their heads some 40 or 50 years' worth of memories. I would listen in amazement as they recalled events from their younger years and wonder how anyone could be that old. Now that I have reached my grandparents' age, I know!

Time is a strange beast. When you are a child, waiting for a treat such as a birthday or Christmas, time drags so very slowly. Yet at some point in adulthood the speed at which time passes goes up a notch. I'm not sure, but I think it happens somewhere around thirty, because suddenly you realise that time is passing so much more quickly than when you were a child. A week is gone in the blink of an eye and birthdays come round about once a quarter rather than once a year. Certainly that's how it seems.

And of course for some towards the end of their lives, time can hang very heavily. For those who are lonely or housebound, a single day can last forever.

There is a book in the Bible called Isaiah and in that book God famously reminds Isaiah that God's ways are very different from the ways of humankind. Certainly God's time is not the same as our time. But what does that mean? Does that mean that God works with a 36-hour day and a 12-day week? No, I don't think so. I think the answer is much more than that.

God loves us and God knows not just what we are doing, but what will happen to us in the future. The result of that knowledge is that God knows best. I can pray to God, offer some specific worry or problem and then I hear nothing. No response, no answer, not even an "I'll get back to you shortly". And sometimes it can take months, even years before I realise that God has answered my prayer, just perhaps not in the way that I expected.

One of the benefits of age is hindsight. As I look back over all the years, yes I can see pain and suffering within my life but – and it's a big but – I can clearly see God guiding me, nurturing me and gently taking me forward. It doesn't explain why bad things happen, maybe that's for a future rambling, but it does help us understand that God does see the bigger picture. God's time is eternity. He has all the time in the world and, unlike us, He knows when the time is right.

Joining the gym

It took me a long time to pluck up the courage to join a gym. Well, I wasn't sure how I would handle being laughed at by all those fit people. Then there was the problem of all my lumps and bumps and rolls of fat. (Where do they come from anyway?) But the gym was running a special promotion of membership for a month and since I am a great one for a bargain and a month didn't sound too life-threatening, I decided to give it a go.

Two things surprised me. First, I found that most other people there were just like me. Sure there were one or two super-fit folk with not an ounce of fat on them anywhere, but I soon discovered that the gym was full of people of all sorts of shapes, sizes and ages, and, secondly, no-one was paying any attention to me: they were all far too busy getting on with their own programmes.

Luckily, there was an instructor who took me around the gym, explaining what all the different pieces of equipment did and how they worked, and suggested what equipment might be best to meet my specific needs.

There are machines that work on every part of your body, from your hips to your back, from your top to your toe, and when you feel completely exhausted, there are mats where you can relax. Over a period of time I hope to lose some weight, but it not just about losing pounds.

What is more important in my book is toning up what I have and becoming fitter.

Like the gym, the Church is full of people of all shapes, sizes and ages. Also like the gym, there is always someone around to help you – explaining what goes on and suggesting different aspects of the Church that might help you in your journey of faith. In a service you can get involved in hymns, readings, prayers and a sermon but, if you are feeling completely exhausted, there is always a spot where you can just sit back and be.

Sometimes we change dramatically when we go to Church, but more often than not it is about working with what we have – toning and strengthening our faith, however small or great that faith may be – and building our strength as a Christian.

The jigsaw puzzle

Rather than just turn up unannounced, I prefer to organise a time of mutual convenience when I'm out visiting members of my congregations. So, I was surprised to find two of my church members extremely tired, particularly as it was only lunchtime. I enquired as to whether they were both well.

"Well, we did have rather a late night last night," they admitted.

"Oh," I replied. "Go anywhere nice?"

They looked slightly embarrassed. "No, we were sitting up trying to do a jigsaw!"

Their admission reminded me of a Laurel and Hardy film I saw years ago. The title has long since disappeared into the mists of time, but I remember that Oliver Hardy was getting married. It was the morning of his wedding and he and the hapless Stan Laurel, on the point of leaving the house, kept being drawn to the uncompleted jigsaw puzzle that lay on the dining room table.

"I'll just put in this piece," seemed to be the continuing comment.

Of course, being a Laurel and Hardy film, the whole situation rapidly deteriorated. The best man turned up to get them to the church and he was soon involved in the jigsaw, as was the priest who also arrived in a state of desperation to try to hurry them along to the service.

Sometimes life seems like a jigsaw puzzle. An amazing assortment of differently shaped pieces, which seem to have no logical connection.

We mentally take out the pieces we understand, the corners, and then we sift through the easy situations – the straight edges. But then there are so many blue pieces which all look the same to make up the sky and elsewhere is such a confusion of colours. Luckily for us jigsaw puzzles generally come with a picture for us to follow but when it comes to our own life, we have to struggle through, often with no obvious idea of where we might be heading.

Sometimes we can fit in several pieces of a puzzle almost at once. Other times we can pour over the uncompleted puzzle for what seems like hours without anything making any sense at all. Doubtless, you can recall occasions in your life when nothing seemed to make any sense but perhaps now, with the benefit of hindsight, you can see the reason behind what happened.

Just remember that God continues to guide us throughout our personal 'jigsaw puzzle'. It may not make any sense to us now, but one day it will.

A muddy walk

I checked the map. Yes, it definitely said Green Lane, but the lane under my feet was far from green. Brown would have been a better description. Thick brown mud! Still, it couldn't go on forever and if I stuck to the middle of the track and tried to step on the grassy mounds, my feet should keep reasonably dry.

Well, that good idea soon went out of the window, as even the grass in the middle of the track became swallowed in squelchy, watery soil and mud. I persevered – after all I had come so far already, it couldn't be much further. And yes, my perseverance was rewarded as I rounded a corner and saw the gate and the end of the track just a few yards away.

But joy at the nearness of the gate soon turned to dismay when I realised what lay in front. The gate itself was half-submerged in thick mud and it was not one gate but two. Two old, very rusty, unsupported metal gates propped up against each other.

I took a moment to take stock. First, I needed to cross over the now-deep muddy track. Then I needed to somehow climb over the gates, even though I knew they would not support my weight. I found a dead twig and tried to use that for support to get me across the track – but that broke and disappeared into the mud. I made the decision to edge gingerly across the bottom rung of the gates so that I could at least cross over the track, but halfway across the gates began to collapse. I fell with them, although I managed to keep upright. Now ankle-deep in mud, my only option was to try to use the now-flattened gates as a kind of cattle grid before they sank completely into the mud.

We meet God in many places. I had not expected to meet God when I was out walking, but back in the safety of home, whilst waiting for my trainers and trousers to wash, I realised just how God had spoken to me. You see, going back, retracing my steps, was never an option. I kept telling myself I had come this far, I would be bound to reach safety soon.

Besides, turning back would have meant going back through all the mud I had just encountered and for what purpose other than failure. Yet having hung on in, just when I thought the end was in sight I was confronted by a huge obstacle – the gate – which caused me physical pain in order to get over it.

Life is a journey. Sometimes – often – the journey is difficult. We find ourselves plodding through the mud, uncertain of the way forward. Indeed, the way forward often appears blocked and we encounter many obstacles on our journey – some of which cause us great pain. But ultimately we arrive, weary and covered with the stains of life's journey, but we do arrive, and we arrive with God.

Making noises

Children, as I have learnt to my cost, are very good mimics. I have certainly experienced huge embarrassment on hearing my children use an expression or a word that I have used, and would rather they had not repeated.

Young children are like sponges – soaking everything up – and this ability to mimic makes a good game.

Ask a child what noise does a dog make and they will happily demonstrate 'woof'. And a sheep, 'baa', and a duck, 'quack'. How about a cow? 'Moo.'

And then there's "What noise does a car make?" "Brrrmmmm!"

So, I was interested in a news item a while ago about electric cars and concerns over their lack of noise. Whilst the sound of traffic can be intrusive, it does serve to let us know that a car, or lorry, or bus, or whatever is coming along – which is a vital piece of information when we are about to cross the road.

But electric cars are silent and researchers at Warwick University are currently investigating what noise they could make so we can hear them coming, which is particularly important to those suffering from any kind of visual impairment.

What's all this got to do with God? Well, it made me ask myself, "What noise does a Christian make?"

Many of the Psalms answer that question. "Praise the Lord. How good it is to sing praises to our God," and the Book of Acts tells us how the early Christians spent their days 'praising the Lord'.

It might not always be easy to praise God in public, but we can at least praise God in our hearts.

Sharpened pencils

Hands up who remembers desks with ink wells at school? Or if you don't remember them, what about fountain pens that had to be filled from a bottle of ink?

When I went to school Biros (the ballpoint pens which take their name from László Bíró, the man who invented them) were strictly taboo. It was a fountain pen or a pencil; I think because handwriting was about style and definition and developing your own characteristics in a way that simply couldn't be achieved with a ballpoint pen.

Then, beyond school, I went to college where I learnt to write shorthand, again with a pencil. Shorthand is about heavy lines and light lines, which require a level of definition which cannot be achieved with a Biro. And to this day, I would much rather write in pencil than use a ballpoint. I enjoy the flexibility that a pencil offers.

Now the lady who takes the minutes of the meetings at one of my churches uses a pencil. Not just one. I'm always impressed that she comes to every meeting equipped with a whole packet of freshly sharpened pencils and as one becomes blunt, she simply swops it for another. Fortunately, I don't think we have yet had a meeting so long that all her pencils have become blunt, because a blunt pencil is of no use for anything, be it writing minutes, taking shorthand or just jotting down notes. But a blunt pencil can be re-sharpened with a pencil sharpener.

People sometimes say to me, "I often wonder where your ramblings are heading!"

We are like pencils. The more work we do, for God, the blunter we become. God is our pencil sharpener. When we engage with God, he sharpens and hones us such that we can go out into the world and be of use, again. As any craftsman knows, a blunt tool is of no use. Stay engaged and therefore sharp with, and for, God.

Using all our senses

My youngest daughter Anne has always liked animals, all sorts of animals from the very large to the very small. She is also an outdoor girl and as a teenager she would help out on a local farm during lambing.

When Anne was lambing you always knew when she was at home because she smelt. Disgusting. Of sheep. Irrespective of whether she left her Wellies outside the front door or not, I knew the minute I walked in not only if Anne was in the house, but also her precise location. It was the sort of smell that hung around, shower and clean clothes or not. I could smell Anne even if I could neither see nor hear her.

At the time of the year when nature bursts into life it is relatively easy to see God in creation. Daffodils, blossom, buds and even lambs are all visual signs of God's presence. But you know God blessed us with five senses. Sight, hearing, taste, touch and smell, and I wonder how well we use even one of them, never mind all five of them, to experience God.

Spring is easy. The 'new life' bit comes as a welcome relief from winter's often-dreary mantel. Yet as the seasons wear on are we sometimes guilty of taking for granted the glory of creation that surrounds us? As these things go, human beings have very good vision. Our range of colours is extensive, but often we only look at the surface.

This was brought home to me when we were on safari in South Africa. The guide would say, "Look, there, through the trees, can you see the...?" I would concentrate and peer into the undergrowth but I couldn't see anything. "You must learn to look into the shrubs, rather than at them."

We cannot see God, nor hear, touch, smell or taste Him. But that shouldn't stop us from using those senses to experience God's presence.

A birthday cake

As part of the celebrations for my fortieth birthday, my sister-in-law made me a cake.

It was fashioned and iced in the shape of a typewriter, because at that time in my life I worked as a secretary and she thought it would be a good representation of me, which of course it was.

Adding artefacts to a celebration cake says a great deal about the person for whom the cake has been made. I suppose now someone making a cake for me would make it in the shape of a Bible, or add one to the decoration.

When I think about it, I have always been a Christian. I was certainly a Christian when I celebrated my fortieth birthday. Yet, in representing my life, my sister-in-law focussed on what I did rather than what I was.

So, here are two questions for you to reflect on:

One: what would you want to see on your celebration cake? What items would tell people about you? And,

Two: if Christianity is an integral part of our lives then shouldn't that be represented somewhere on the cake as well, even if we don't 'do it' for a job?

We often refer to the 'secular' and the 'religious'. Yet surely the two should complement each other. Surely we can be a Christian gardener, teacher, student, nurse, etc.

Christianity isn't something we only do on a Sunday, nor should our faith's only representation be a cross around our necks or a fish on the back of our car. Christianity should be an integral part of our everyday lives and we shouldn't have to tell people we are Christians - it should be obvious.

Putting others first

Blackie (that's my dog) and I have been living together for around two and half years. I've never had a dog before so, for me at least, it has been a steep learning curve.

On the whole I would say Blackie is a good dog – he's easy to get on with, has a nice temperament, and gets on well with both humans and other dogs. He doesn't need too much exercise and he's good company. But what I have learnt is that the dog has needs. He needs food – obviously. He needs to be walked – fair enough. He likes a certain amount of fuss and cuddles – don't we all? But it's more than that. My life has changed since the arrival of the dog. I have to think in advance. I can't just go away overnight without some kind of forward planning for the dog. I can't leave him in the car if the weather is too hot. I can't leave him on his own for hours at a time. In order for our relationship to work well, I have to consider his needs, sometimes before my own.

And sometimes he takes things that I considered to be mine - like the cheese!

But all in all, he is a comfort and a joy in my life and I wouldn't be without him. A bit like God, really. Because once you invite God into your life, things change. There are times when you have to put God's needs before your own and there are also times when God takes away something that you thought was yours! But in establishing a two-way relationship with God, in return I have received comfort, love and richness in my life that I never knew existed.

Coming up slowly

I'm not really that much of a swimmer, although I can swim a passable length, and I am certainly no diver, but I do know about the dangers of the bends. If a diver tries to reach the surface too quickly following a deep dive, bubbles of gases from their lungs can enter their joints, and even their brain, causing all sorts of unpleasant effects which can be fatal if not treated in an appropriate fashion. It certainly necessitates spending hours in a decompression chamber.

But knowing the risks, why would a diver try to reach the surface too quickly? I suppose the most obvious reason is lack of air, either due to a fault in their equipment or a poor judgement of time, so that their air supply is about to run out.

We all have times of crisis in our lives, and sometimes the crises we go through send us to the very bottom of a pit: the darkest place in our lives. A place from which we long to escape as quickly as possible, so that we can once again feel the sun's warmth on our face and breathe with ease.

Although it may be very hard to understand at the time, there is often a good reason for what we are experiencing. Not that God wants us to suffer pain, but there is a learning curve within what we are going through and from that learning curve comes strength and courage, which will enhance our lives in the future.

Whilst we are trying to come back up it can so often feel like one step forward and two back, but we need to move slowly and gently, trying to allow things to happen in God's time, which is never, ever the same as our time.

"The slower we come back up, the better our recovery" is something which was said to me very recently and is what prompted these ramblings.

When you find yourself at the bottom, recover slowly, recover well and recover with God at your side.

Remembering names

I make no secret of the fact that I'm not terribly good at remembering names. I know some people can absorb and recall names without difficulty, even months after an initial introduction. But for me, it takes ages. So the task of remembering the names of more than 150 boys when I was involved in a school chaplaincy and teaching Religious Education presented me with a challenge.

In order to get to know them better, I began by asking them to share with me the name of their hero or role model. As you might expect, sports personalities featured high up on their list, as did such folk as dads, granddads and even older and younger siblings. It became obvious that their admiration was seeded in such attributes as courage, being a good team player and doing your best for yourself and your country.

So I gave all the boys two options. Either I would to get to know them because they were polite, helpful, and keen to learn or I would get to know them because they were a pain in the neck. Naturally, they all opted for the first option. Equally I was not at all surprised that the majority of the first names I started to remember were the ones of the naughty boys.

But it begs the question: For what would you like to be remembered? What will be your legacy not just for your children, but the society in which you live?

Being in ministry means I am often called upon to lead funerals. On every occasion, whether the deceased was known to me or not, I am interested as to what family and friends have to say about the person who has died and it always leaves me wondering what people will say about me when I am no more.

It is one thing to stand before God and have Him say, "Well done, thou good and faithful servant," but even after your death, memory of your Earthly life will live on. Now is a good time to decide what you would like that memory to be.

Walking the dog

I have to walk the dog twice a day. Well, I suppose I don't have to, but Blackie sort of expects it. So we go out first thing in the morning around the village for about 20 minutes and then after lunch we generally take off towards the edge of the village and beyond. Sometimes we cut across the fields but, more often than not, the dog and I mooch along for about 20 minutes before turning around and coming back home.

And because there isn't a huge amount of conversation between the dog and me – other than, "Blackie! Come on!" or "You've already sniffed that bush three times, you really don't need to go back to it again!" – I tend to use my dog walking time as thinking time. Especially the afternoon walk, since once we clear the houses I don't often meet anyone else.

So, the other afternoon, the dog and I were wandering along and I was struggling with an idea for the first part of the service. Sometimes ideas just come and sometimes they don't and this was a 'don't' situation. Anyway, I was playing with some thoughts and gradually an idea began to take shape. So I mentally worked on it a bit more, fleshing out my initial thoughts until I had pretty much decided how it would come together and fit neatly in with the sermon.

I was so deep in thought that I hadn't realised just how far we had walked and was suddenly jolted back to the reality that Blackie and I had wandered much further along the lane than we had ever done before. Not only had we discovered pastures new, but the view was amazing and well worth the extra walk home.

God has a habit of wanting to take us to places that we haven't been. That can be scary, but the view – what He shows us when we get there – can be truly spectacular and well worth the hard work.

What's in your bag?

I recently did a school assembly about going on a journey. I took two bags, one full of goodies relevant to an overnight trip, pyjamas, wash kit, a book to read, a change of clothes, some food and, of course, a cuddly toy – the other a bag for my journey with God.

Having asked the children to guess what items I might have put in my overnight bag, I then asked them to suggest what I might have in my God bag.

"A Bible," was perhaps a fairly predictable response. They were amazed when I opened the bag and revealed its contents. Nothing. It was completely empty. Not even a Bible!

I explained that in order to journey with God we must keep our bag empty, ready for God to fill it with what He desired. It is all too easy for us to fill our God bag with clutter. Grumpy moods, a grudge, a selfish desire to have what we want, all take up precious space. The truly amazing thing about God is He is constantly looking to give us things. His love, His peace, a sense of wellbeing, skills and talents that we can use in His service. Yet we cannot hope to receive anything if our bag is full to bursting with rubbish.

Just think of the rubbish you collect in your pocket, your handbag, or your car. Sweet wrappers, empty crisp packets, used car park tickets, broken pens – no doubt you can add many more. And if you collect all that in things that you regularly use, what then have you collected in your God bag? In fact, when did you last open your God bag and check its contents?

Maybe the summer, with all its promise of holidays, relaxation and enjoyment and the associated packing and unpacking is a good time to check your God bag. You may be surprised at the amount of rubbish you have collected without realising it. You may also be surprised to find what God has put in there when you weren't looking.

Changing fashions

One thing guaranteed to liven up an otherwise dull couple of hours and prompt instant hilarity is to spend some time browsing lovingly through an old photograph album, especially in the company of those belonging to the next generation down from you.

"Mum, what on Earth are you wearing?" or "Gosh, just look at Dad with hair!" does nothing for your personal ego, but certainly highlights the fact that things change. Fashions, hairstyles, even the shape of spectacles are all good pointers as to the date the photo was taken. Tank tops, bellbottoms, flares, drainpipes, winkle-pickers and beehive hairstyles all conjure up special memories, but also a certain amount of "Did I really wear that? How embarrassing!"

Of course, at the time, we were the height of fashion, but now even we would rather forget some of the things the photos remind us of.

Mind you, it's not just fashions that change. Everything changes. Our homes – both the style and the content. (Who remembers icicles on the inside of your bedroom window and black-and-white television?) Our cars. Our leisure. Even our food packaging is constantly being updated. We are always on the move, or at least the life that surrounds us is always changing, sometimes without us hardly noticing.

But there is one thing that doesn't change. There is one thing that remains constant in our lives and that is God. His love for us does not alter. No matter who we are, what we do, how we think and even whether God holds a place of prominence in our lives or we totally ignore Him, He loves us with a strength and a consistency that is beyond belief.

Recycling our "rubbish"

Any good gardener worth his or her fruit, flowers and vegetables will tell you the value of good feeding and, in particular, making sure that the roots of a plant are firmly enclosed in a good compost.

We keep a compost bin in the garden, which is the final resting place for all the kitchen scraps. Well, I have to admit that the two rabbits eat any leftover or unwanted greens, along with apple cores and carrot peelings, but the remainder – the orange peel, onion skins, dead flowers and the clippings from the garden – all find their way to the compost.

I do not have a particularly scientific brain so I do not really understand how it is that whilst I put orange peel and dead flowers in the top, I extract from the bottom a wonderfully dark brown, crumbly compost, which is so life-giving to my garden. Yes, I know it has something to do with worms and enzymes and things like that, but in the main I regard it as one of life's mysteries that something which would otherwise be classed as rubbish can become instrumental to growth and new life.

I learn a lot from nature and from my garden and there is, I believe, much to be learnt from the process of composting.

Instead of allowing ourselves to be completely overwhelmed and bogged down by all the rubbish, all the things we have done wrong, all the mistakes we have made, all the seemingly useless things in our lives; if only we can give them to God, He will turn them into a medium which is rich in life-giving support.

At Easter, when Jesus died on the cross, He took all the rubbish in our lives and, through the resurrection, went through the most amazing transformation so that we too could be fed with new life and enjoy new growth.

Jesus died that we might live and live on into eternity.

Keeping your options open

My youngest daughter, Anne, always wanted to be a vet. Not the fluffy bunny variety. No, Anne is well aware that there is more to being a vet than playing with fluffy kittens. When she was nine, Anne took a voluntary job at a local stables helping to muck out and generally look after the horses and from there she progressed to working Saturdays in a veterinary practice.

Of course, she always knew it would be difficult to get into, but Anne was very determined. She got good GCSE results and as she approached her A-levels she would spend every available moment getting as much hands-on experience as she could. She even spent one holiday taking part in a course that involved being called out in the middle of the night to attend a mock case. Now, there's dedication for you.

And I have no doubt Anne would have made a good vet. She has a real rapport with animals. Animals big or small respond to Anne and she has a gentleness about her that, coupled with a caring attitude and a tough streak, would have stood her in good stead. But, as I have already said, the way into veterinary science is tough. To even be considered for a place at university you must have three A-grade A-levels and, sadly, Anne's grades were not of sufficient standard. So Anne, having been offered a conditional place dependent upon her results, was turned down.

Rejection, of course, is always painful, but more than that came the challenge of, if not veterinary medicine then what should she do? What career should she follow? Anne still doesn't know. She has accepted a place at Heriot-Watt University in Edinburgh to study for a degree in biological science, but where it will take her she has absolutely no idea. The staff there advise her that it is a good all-round degree which will leave lots of doors open for her: food hygiene, marine biology, brewing and distilling, to name but some, but ultimately Anne is now travelling down a road without any clue as to her destination.

So why am I telling you all this? Because, every so often, we can end up following a very narrow course, with only one aim in mind. For God this is not good, because we need to be open: not just to listen to God, but also to have about us a flexibility that allows God to mould us and a faith to be led by God into the unknown.

That's hard. Our nature is to want answers and to know where we are going before we start. Yet in order to serve God to the best of our ability, we must be prepared to go where God leads us without answers and certainly without a map. The more open our minds, the wider our vision and the wider our vision, the more use we are to God.

Jagged edges

I had occasion to have a meeting with a firm of solicitors the other day. One of the things we were talking about was deeds. Not deeds that we do, but deeds of houses. She was telling me how years ago, deeds were written by hand, in duplicate, on a large sheet of parchment. One copy of the deeds was set out on the left hand side of the page and the other on the right. Having completed the exercise the page was then cut in half, but not with a straight cut. The cut was made in a random jagged pattern – with good reason.

In the fullness of time if someone wanted to be certain that the copy of the deeds to hand was a genuine copy, it would be matched with the original held by the solicitors. Only if the jagged edges matched exactly would the copy be certified as true.

I have to say there was something about that idea which spoke to me. I like to think that we have that kind of relationship with God.

We are, of course, all made in the image of God but we are also unique. We are all special. We are all different. We all have jagged edges. But I hope at the final day of judgement, when we stand before God, God just might in his infinite wisdom and graciousness invite us to stand next to him and see if our jagged edges match His. If they do, then the gift of eternity will be ours.

We are made in the image of God – more than that we are part of God's original plan.

Losing sight of God

I do try very hard to rise to challenges, especially ones that take me outside my comfort zone. Of course, that doesn't mean I'm always successful – far from it – but my aim is to at least consider something rather than immediately dismiss it out of hand.

I think one of my greatest challenges was to walk the Inca Trail. A good friend of mine was looking for a walking partner and, in a moment of weakness, I agreed.

It wasn't the distance that bothered me. I was pretty confident that with sensible training I could achieve the 26 mile trek. No, it was the altitude. The Inca Trail ascends to a height in excess of 16,000 feet (5,000 metres), and on a previous trip to South America I had suffered badly from altitude sickness at a much lower altitude, so I was more than a little concerned. But I decided to face my fear and begin training. Training involved swimming and extra walking.

One evening, when I was out walking, I heard the familiar hiss of a hot air balloon. The site of hot air balloons drifting across a warm, late evening sky was not uncommon, but this balloon was particularly low. Hauling its bulk just above the Hindhead traffic lights, the huge red balloon was obviously close to landing. It was unmissable, barely clearing the tops of the surrounding trees.

The balloon disappeared in the general direction of Grayshott and I turned the corner and headed down the Tilford Road, only to be stopped by the balloon's recovery vehicle.

"Excuse me," said a rather worried looking driver. "Have you seen a hot air balloon? I seem to have lost it."

How anyone could lose sight of something so big is a mystery. Yet God is very big and we can very easily lose sight of Him. Like the balloon somewhere in front of the driver, God goes before us. But then something gets in our way and our contact with God is lost.

If that happens to you, don't panic. Ask for help. Pray. And if you still can't find God, then just relax and let God find you.

The Christmas amaryllis

I honestly can't remember when it started and I certainly don't know how or why, but the tradition of giving and receiving an amaryllis plant between my two daughters - Ruth and Anne - and myself, has become as much a part of Christmas as roast turkey, crackers and Christmas pudding. I buy one for Ruth, Ruth buys one for Anne and Anne buys one for me so that each one of us has an amaryllis plant to nurture and grow in January.

Of course, as with every other plant, different growers suggest different ways.I always start mine off in the airing cupboard, even though the instructions on the packet say place it in the light. But whichever way you start them off, I find the humble amaryllis plant truly amazing. Within days the pointed tip emerges, after which you can almost see the stem growing and that stem continues to grow and grow and grow – generally at least 18 inches before the flower starts to open.

Unlike so many other plants, the bud stay tight shut – not even a suggestion of opening – until the stem reaches its fullness of height. Then, and only then, right at the end of its journey does the flower open and the true beauty of the plant is finally revealed.

I'm not sure when the human body reaches its peak – probably somewhere around the early twenties – but I do know that as we journey through life we gradually deteriorate, particularly physically. Yet as Christians, we believe that our life on Earth is simply part of the journey towards that which lies beyond – eternity.

So rather than be downhearted and struggle to come to terms with the ageing process, perhaps we should take strength from nature, particularly the amaryllis, which is at its most beautiful at the end of its journey.

God doesn't look at the outer self – the wrinkles, the grey hair, the physical signs of age. Rather God sees the ultimate beauty that will only become apparent when our journey here has ended.

Enjoy your journey, travel it well, and just like the amaryllis, keep growing up, towards God.

The innocence of a child

Anyone who has ever had anything to do with children, especially young children, will be aware of just how good kids can be at causing you embarrassment. Children seem to arrive with a well-honed talent for saying just the wrong thing, at the wrong time, in a particularly loud voice, leaving those in charge of them with very red faces.

This happened at one of my churches just recently. It was during Communion. Here, in the United Reformed Church, we use bread rather than wafers. A large slice of bread is broken and placed on the plate (or plates) holding tiny squares of bread, and these plates are then taken around the congregation for them to take a piece.

Of course, we who are grown-ups know that etiquette says you take a small piece of bread, which you hold quietly in your hand until you are invited to eat it, which is also done in total silence.

But Charlie didn't know that – why should he? There are lots of things that a three(ish) year-old doesn't yet know. So, when the plate comes around, Charlie takes the big piece. From where I was standing at the front of the church I could see his mum flush with embarrassment. It was one of those 'I wish the ground would swallow me up' moments. But worse was to come. Having eaten the bread Charlie then exclaimed in a very loud voice, "Mmm, yummy!"

Needless to say, mum was full of apologies after the service. But you know, I think Charlie got it right and it is we grown-ups who need to learn. Because as I see it, the whole business of Communion, of receiving bread and wine, is to remind ourselves of Jesus' great love for us – a love that involved the giving of his life. And maybe we should be keener to receive a big chunk of that love rather than the tiny piece that we usually take.

And just as Charlie clearly made his enjoyment known, so should we.

Jesus calls us to share what we know – go and make disciples of all people – and Jesus also said we should be as children. Now I don't think that means going back to temper tantrums and nappies, but I do think it sometimes means saying it with the innocence of a child. Telling other people just how Jesus makes us feel.

Being in control

My eldest daughter Ruth and her partner Jonno got married last July. They got married in a barn in Sussex: a civil ceremony followed by a blessing. (I did the blessing and I was very excited!) After the formal ceremony, we went into the courtyard for coffee whilst the room was prepared for food, and after the food that same room housed a barn dance.

Of course, things are a lot different these days. When I married, I married from home and my mum and dad were heavily involved in all the preparations.

These days with so many couples already sharing their lives it is often the couple themselves who carry out the bulk of the arrangements, and certainly this is how it was for Ruth and Jonno. Yes, I went with Ruth to help her choose her wedding dress, but things such as flowers, catering and seating arrangements had all been organised by the couple themselves.

Understandably, Ruth wanted everything to be perfect, not just for her and Jonno, but also for the guests, and she wanted to be in control. In the nicest possible way, she wanted to be at the barn on the morning of the wedding, supervising the flowers and the lights and the arrangement of the cupcakes, but she couldn't because she was busy having her hair and make-up beautifully done and being dressed by her mum and her bridesmaid.

I kept telling her, it would all be fine, but she just wanted to double-check, and she found it increasingly frustrating to have to let go and let other people take responsibility.

Letting go – letting someone else do something that either we know we are good at, or we want to do ourselves – is never easy. But letting go achieves two things. It encourages trust – trust in someone else, and it encourages growth – encouraging someone else to develop and achieve his or her own potential. And it removes some of the worry and responsibility from our lives.

Just before he died, Jesus put a towel around his waist and, like a servant, washed his disciples' feet. That simple action teaches us two things.

1. We must learn how to serve other people, and

2. Sometimes we must allow other people to serve us.

We all have gifts and skills and we should use these gifts and skills for the good of other people, but we must learn to stand back sometimes so that we can encourage and enable the gifts and skills of others.

(In case you're wondering, it was an amazing day and everything went just fine.)

Black teeth

Having been born and bred in the south of England, I am still enjoying getting to know other parts of the country. Suffolk is one of those areas that I am largely unfamiliar with, so it was particularly good to spend a week there recently on holiday.

We were based in a caravan near Lowestoft so we enjoyed beach walks, a brewery and, amongst other things, a whole day in Lowestoft and in particular several hours in the Elizabethan museum. I enjoy history and I am always fascinated by visual displays. This particular museum offered plenty of room-by-room displays, but also an ongoing audio presentation to explain in more detail the things you could see.

So, we moved around through living and sleeping accommodation ending up in the room that housed the shop. Unusually the audiotape didn't end in the shop, but continued to explain the kind of foods that the Elizabethans would have eaten. Sugar had just arrived from the colonies, but it was very expensive and, therefore, only within the budget of the very rich. It soon became clear to those very rich who could afford sugar, that this amazing new food substance turned your teeth black!

Of course, today such a revelation would send you running to the dentist, but in the Elizabethan era black teeth were considered a sign of wealth and the height of fashion! So much so that the poorer people who couldn't afford sugar would deliberate blacken their teeth to give others the impression that they were wealthy.

In my kitchen I have a mug that says, 'Lead me not into temptation, I can find it for myself.' Temptation presents itself in many forms not least the whims and fancies of the current fashion. And fashions, as we know, come and go. What was considered the thing to do in Elizabethan England is now the exact opposite of what we strive to achieve. Today we want pearly white teeth – that has become the hallmark, if you like, of beauty and wealth.

It is easy to be led astray by the world. To help us, God gives us guidelines as to how we should live our lives. Those guidelines are called the Ten Commandments. They were given to Moses many, many, many years ago but the principles hold true even for today. Don't kill, don't steal, be respectful to others and, most important of all, put God in a place of priority in your life.

Honeymoon gifts

As many of you will know, Jeff and I got married in September. We had an amazing day, surrounded by our families and our friends, as well as our friends from the four pastorate churches. The day was fun; the reception included afternoon tea as well as a jazz band and early on the morning after the wedding, we set off on our honeymoon.

We wanted to visit a place where neither of us had previously been so we chose Indonesia. We flew to Lombok and after five days transferred to Bali, where we spent the remainder of our two weeks.

Of course, we always knew it would be special. Not just because it was our honeymoon, but because it was an amazing opportunity to travel to, and experience, cultures and ways of life far different from our own. (As well of course, as temperatures in the upper 30s which was also a lot different to the temperature we had left behind in England!)

It soon became clear that because we were on honeymoon we received various gifts from the different places where we stayed. These gifts ranged from a bottle of bubbly, a "honeymoon cake" a wooden figure and beautiful flower arrangements on our bed to towels shaped into animals.

My favourite had to be the two swans, one male and one female, placed beak to beak on our bed, such that the two heads and necks formed a heart shape.

I didn't really want to disturb them but as I gently tried to move them it became clear that one was supporting the other. Without each other's help, they simply fell apart.

In any relationship, but particularly in marriage one partner needs to support the other. However, whether we are married or not, we are in a relationship, a partnership with God and just like the swans, if we move away from God, we fall apart.

The dog and the cushion

Blackie, my dog, isn't allowed on the sofa. It's a house rule. We don't have many house rules: just three. Blackie isn't allowed on the beds, he isn't allowed to come to the table when we are eating, and he isn't allowed on the sofa. Generally he's pretty good. Except, that is, when he's home alone. As soon as he thinks we've gone out, he seems to think the rules no longer apply.

Keeping him off the beds is down to us making sure the bedroom doors are shut and putting something in front of the doors that don't shut properly, otherwise our highly inventive dog will push the door until it opens. But the sofa is a different matter altogether. When we are out, Blackie has access to the lounge – that's where he has his bed – so there is nothing to stop him ignoring the house rule and making himself comfortable on the sofa. Which he does every time we go out.

How do I know? Because whenever he gets on the sofa, he pushes the cushions off. So cushions on floor mean dog has been on sofa. Of course, he denies his misdemeanour every time, coming up with foolish excuses such as the wind blew the cushions off or West Haddon suffered a small earthquake whilst we were out. But I know exactly what he's been up to.

However, he got his comeuppance just before Christmas. We came home and, as usual, he raced to the door to greet us (and cover up the fact that once again the cushions were on the floor and he had been on the sofa). Except this time in pushing the cushions off, he had managed to catch the threads from one of the cushions in his collar, so when he appeared at the door 'wearing' a cushion around his neck, he was unable to hide his wrongdoing.

We often do things that we know are wrong, but we think that if we pretend, then God doesn't know. But He does know. Just as I know what Blackie has been up to by the evidence I see, so God knows what naughty things we have been up to by the evidence God sees. Just like me turning a blind eye to Blackie, God can "turn a blind eye" to us but there are times, as Blackie discovered, when the truth of what we have done wrong cannot be denied.

God loves us, just as I love my dog but the rules are there for a reason and God knows when we break them. I doubt I will change my dog, but we can change. We can at least do our best to follow God's rules.

Teaching Murphy recall

My youngest daughter Anne has acquired a dog: Murphy. He's a Collie cross. I'm not sure what he's crossed with, and he doesn't look anything like a Collie to me, but then I'm not really a dog person, so I wouldn't really know.

Anyway, Murphy is an RSPCA rescue puppy and Anne and her partner Chris are working hard to train him. He came house-trained, so that's a bonus, but at the moment he doesn't go off the lead and they are trying to teach him recall. Although they don't have a large garden, they do have a park nearby so they put Murphy on a very long lead in the park and if he comes back when they call him, he gets a treat.

It's a good plan and it's working well, except Murphy is now getting wise to this, so he rushes back, grabs the treat and then rushes off again. He hasn't yet grasped the concept of 'stay' then! Even though he knows he'll get a treat if he comes back, if he's got a better offer – like another dog to sniff or a duck to chase – then no amount of calling will encourage him to return.

In many ways our relationship with God involves treats. When we come back to God, he doesn't reward us with presents but with presence. He offers His love, His companionship, His care and His concern for our welfare as He walks the journey with us.

But the life of a Christian can be hard and the world can offer many temptations, which at the time might just seem like a better offer. Money, power, greed, are all things that can be appealing at the time, but they don't last.

Eventually the duck that Murphy is chasing will fly away or the other dog he's sniffing will go home. But Anne and Chris will stay there calling Murphy until he comes back.

Which is just how it is for us and God. The God who loves us will keep calling us until finally we return to Him and He takes us home.